Planning for Staff and Support Units

by Rochelle O'Connor
Senior Research Associate

A Research Report from The Conference Board

Ministry of Education, Ontario
Information Centre, 13th Floor,
Mowat Block, Queen's Park,
Toronto, Ont.   M7A 1L2

658
.401
O 18

Contents

	Page
WHY THIS REPORT	v
INTRODUCTION	1
1. PREPARATION OF STAFF UNIT PLANS	2
When All Corporate Staff Units Prepare Plans	2
When Only Some Corporate Staff Units Prepare Plans	3
Planning by Division and Subsidiary Staff Units	4
When Plans Are Not Required	4
2. THE STAFF UNIT PLANNING PROCESS	6
Types of Plans Required	6
Scheduling and Integrating Staff Plans	7
Measurement Criteria for Staff Unit Plans	9
3. CONTENTS OF STAFF AND SUPPORT UNIT PLANS	11
Most Common Items in Plan Contents	11
Less Prevalent Elements	18
4. APPRAISING STAFF UNIT PLANNING	23
Benefits Perceived	23
Doubts and Drawbacks	24

Table

1. Prevalence of Staff Unit Planning Requirements ... 3

Exhibits

1. Planning Process Suggestions for Corporate Staff Departments
   —A Food Company ... 8
2. Schedule of Planning Cycle—A Hotel and Restaurant Chain ... 9
3. Instructions for Completing Integrated Plan for Staff Groups
   —A Wood Products Manufacturer ... 12
4. Format for Developing Staff Department Plans
   —An Electric Utility ... 14
5. Guidelines and Instructions for Corporate Staff Department Plan
   —An Industrial Products Manufacturer ... 16
6. Definitions of Objectives, Goals and Action Plans for Staff Units
   —A Chemical Manufacturing Company ... 17
7. Instructions for Developing Fundamental Purposes Statement of Staff Unit
   —A Hotel and Restaurant Chain ... 18
8. Example of Format for Strategy Summary
   —A Bank's Data Processing Department ... 19
9. Example of Plan Summary and Format for Monitoring
   —A Fuel Supplier's Public Affairs Unit ... 20
10. Manpower and Expense Forecast Form for Staff Units
    —An Industrial Engineering Firm ... 21

Why This Report

PLANNING, an evolving corporate function, has been a major item on The Conference Board's research agenda over the past decade. This is the fourteenth planning-related research report since 1972.

In the Fall of 1979, the Board organized a Panel of Planning Executives. Its members are surveyed twice each year on topics of current concern.

The focus of this survey is on planning by corporate staff and support units. Although these groups do not have a direct profit responsibility, they make substantial contributions to the company's progress and, therefore, are already an integral part of planning in many firms.

The planning requirements for these units often call for specialized treatment. For this and many other reasons, many planning directors question their usefulness. On the other hand, neglecting the needs and priorities of these units can lead to difficulties for those who rely on their services. The Board is grateful to the members of the Panel who contributed their thoughts on the substance of these two viewpoints.

JAMES T. MILLS
President

Introduction

THE ROLE of staff and support unit plans in the corporate planning system has been accorded little attention in the larger framework of developing strategy and positioning the corporation and its business units in their competitive environments. The effort and time involved in the normal planning cycle have frequently been quite enough to occupy the energies of managers and planning staffs, and the support areas have received casual notice. At a number of companies, as a matter of fact, requiring staff groups to write plans and integrating them with the plans of operating units have never even been seriously considered.

Nevertheless, the services provided by many of these groups can significantly affect company operations, and there are evident dangers in ignoring their needs and requests. Therefore, many firms make staff and support unit plans an integral part of overall plans.

Whether the exercise is worth the candle is questioned by many planning directors who find that the planning requirements for these units often call for special handling and understanding. The usefulness of staff plans varies greatly among companies, and they are judged accordingly.

The planners who participated in this survey offer their candid comments and views on staff unit planning. Most of them do have such requirements and a bank vice president expresses the rationale:

"While the development of staff unit plans does not benefit so directly from the application of traditional strategic planning concepts as do line unit (profit center) plans, these staff unit plans are indispensable elements of the process and key contributors to the strategy which evolves at the corporate level. The value of the communication realized in the development of staff unit plans is significant; the economy of the lines of business and of the corporation is brought to the consciousness of both line executives and corporate executives by this mandated interchange. Moreover, the planning process (in either the operational or strategic phase) can provide the mechanism for enabling important trade-offs to take place in a suitable environment and time frame; in this way, line units exercise a degree of control over staff unit overheads and staff units may exact the kind of resources that they require to provide the quality and quantity of desired support."

As part of its continuing program of corporate planning research, The Conference Board surveys a panel of leading planning executives twice a year on subjects of current interest to corporate planners. This survey addresses some of the issues concerning planning for staff and support units (e.g., human resources, law, purchasing, data processing, public affairs): those entities without profit responsibility whose function it is to provide advice, render service, or exercise control in behalf of corporate or business unit management. This is the fifth survey in the series, and is based on responses from eighty-five companies.

Chapter 1
Preparation of Staff Unit Plans

OF THE 85 COMPANIES in the survey, 80 reported on their requirements for *corporate* staff unit plans; the other five supplied information *only* for their *business units, divisions or subsidiaries.* A total of 28 companies provided material on such business unit staff plans.

As Table 1 shows, 58, or almost three-quarters of the 80 companies commenting on the practice, require some or all of their *corporate* staff and support units to prepare written plans. Plan preparation is more prevalent among the participating nonmanufacturing companies—banks, insurance companies, utilities, retail firms, and other types of service companies—than among the manufacturers.

Special conditions in the company or industry sometimes influence staff unit planning. For instance, when a transportation leasing firm initiated a management by objectives (MBO) program as a basis for its incentive compensation plan, each department head was obliged to set objectives for the unit. Thus, the written staff unit plans that had been discretionary before the MBO program became mandatory.

Staff unit planning in an electric utility in New York State receives impetus from a state-mandated general management audit every five years. "In preparation for this audit," the planning director states, "we ask all of our departments to prepare five-year strategic planning documents that summarize any changes in planning practices and long-range (two to five year) goals."

When All Corporate Staff Units Prepare Plans

In the companies that require all of their corporate staff units to prepare written plans, it is not unusual to find variations in the kinds of plans they are asked to submit. Thus, a diversified manufacturer, whose fifteen centralized staff units provide operational and strategic support to its six operating profit centers worldwide, reports:

"All staff units do prepare strategic plans in response to operations and corporate-level needs. The more detailed planning, reduced to writing, will be developed by the following groups: Corporate Technology and Venture Management; Advertising and Marketing Services; Economic Research, Corporate Planning and Marketing Research, and Marketing Development; Employee Relations; and Business Information Services. Other staff units may not choose to write a detailed report."

Several planners point out that some staff units are deemed of greater importance than others in their contribution to the company's overall strategy or operations. They are often charged to develop plans that cover a longer time span, or that address strategic implications. This is true, for example, for the human resources and data-processing functions in a number of companies. Research and development may be critical to technology companies. In others, the corporate facilities department makes a substantive contribution to the plans of business units and the corporation as a whole.

Two panel participants describe the varying emphases placed on the plans of the corporate staff units in their companies:

"All of the staff units prepare written plans. Some are little more than budgets, while others are detailed written plans. Those with more comprehensive plans tend to be the staff groups that charge their service to the operations, like information systems, research and engineering; others, like tax, treasurer and law departments are absorbed at the corporate level."

—*A forest products company*

* * *

"All of our staff units are required to prepare written plans, including both operating (one-year horizon with budget included) and strategic (five-year horizon) plans. In the case of the strategic plans, staff units prepare response plans providing details as to the feasibility, timing and resources required to support the line depart-

Table 1: Prevalence of Staff Unit Planning Requirements

Staff Units that Plan	Number of Companies Reporting									
	Corporate Staffs						Business Unit Staffs		
	Manufacturing		Nonmanufacturing		Total		Manu-facturing	Nonmanu-facturing	Total
	Number	Percent[1]	Number	Percent[1]	Number	Percent[1]	Number	Number	Number
All required	24	48	19	66	43	54	10	4	14
Some required	9	18	6	21	15	19	1	2	3
None required	18	35	4	14	22	28	4	1	5
Discretionary	—	—	—	—	—	—	5	1	6
Total	51		29		80		20	8	28

[1] Percentages do not add to 100 because of rounding.

ments' strategic plans. Obviously, for some staff departments (i.e., human resources, or information management and research), this step requires considerably more effort than for others (i.e., auditing, whose volume and nature of work is not as extensively affected by strategic plans)."

—*A bank*

When Only Some Corporate Staff Units Prepare Plans

In companies requiring only some corporate staff units to prepare plans, the units that must do so are selected for different reasons. Many of the planning executives say that the size of the staff or support unit is one of the principal factors that determines whether or not it should prepare written plans. Another factor considered in this decision is the size of the unit's expense budget or its capital needs.

But a more significant key to the selection of units for planning is the relative importance of the unit's support efforts to the line operations of the company, or to corporate strategy. This factor provides for a disparate array of required staff unit plans among the survey respondents, reflecting the different needs of different types of businesses (see box).

A bank vice president observes of his organization's practice:

"The deciding factor for staff plan development is its strategic necessity in the achievement of the corporate objectives and in the implementation of line-unit strategies. The importance of the other staff units to *significantly* influence the business success of the corporation through either strategic or tactical planning is *relatively* minimal and not considered worth the time to develop, review, approve and monitor their plans."

Planners from financial institutions, in particular, perceive the work of some staff units as critical to the organization as a whole. To illustrate:

- At an insurance company, the actuarial, legal and data-processing units prepare plans because, according to its spokesman, "Actuaries design and price our products; counsel interprets the substantial impact of regulatory agencies on markets, products and operations generally; and data-processing units provide the arteries for the flow in information, funds and records."

- A bank planner explains that the four key support areas that are now required to develop strategic plans (an evolution from the previous practice of asking all staff units to prepare an annual business plan) are marketing, treasury, government affairs, and human resources. They deal with the four critical bank resources—products, funding, influence and labor management. "The four

---

Disparity of Planning Requirements for Corporate Staff Units

Here are two examples of selectivity regarding corporate staff unit plan preparation:

Plans Required	Plans Not Required
Systems and data processing	Personnel
Merchandise (buying)	Public affairs
Marketing	Legal
Real estate	Controllers
Credit	Audit

—*A department store chain*

* * *

Plans Required	Plans Not Required
Personnel	Aviation
Legal	Other small units
Treasurer	
Comptroller	
Corporate relations	

—*A business information publisher*

PREPARATION OF STAFF UNIT PLANS

areas are major cogs in the business wheel alongside the line units. Consequently, it is important for them to plan in response not only to the line unit needs, but also to larger forces within the corporation."

• Another banker cites the data-processing department, the development and implementation of whose plan "has major ramifications on the implementation of many business unit strategic plans, because its completion is paramount to implementation of new products."

Planning by Division and Subsidiary Staff Units

So far as planning requirements are mandated for divisional staff units, if centralized corporate functions exist, they usually control this requirement. This is true, for example, for a textile manufacturer with a small corporate staff, whose data processing, transportation and engineering departments are centralized; and some manufacturing companies have a centralized research and development organization.

In many companies with divisional staffs, the operating unit manager decides what the planning responsibilities will be for the staff units. Several of the responding planning executives state that they are not sure how the operating units structure the preparation of their annual plans, or whether the staff units actually develop written plans, which are then incorporated into the business unit plan.

Here is how the planning executive of a large industrial products manufacturing company describes divisional staff unit planning in his company:

"The strategic planning system does require certain division staff functions to prepare functional support plans. Corporate functional staffs for engineering, production operations, personnel organization and management development, and information systems each administer a functional support planning process for their functional counterparts in the division organization, as part of the overall strategic planning system. As with the strategic planning system, the hierarchy of plans builds from business segment plans to division plans and operations plans. An attempt is made to integrate these five-plus year plans into an overall corporate level plan, particularly in the engineering and production operations (manufacturing) functions.

"The marketing, finance and international staffs, as well as transportation, law, purchasing, and so on, are not required to prepare functional support plans by their corporate counterparts. The division general manager, as the chief strategic planner, may involve those functions in the strategic planning process in his division. Those functions may have a substantial involvement in major strategic action programs which implement the business segment and division strategies; however, the general manager and his strategic planner are the ones to decide if

---

Disillusionment with Zero-Base Budgeting

Two companies in the survey subjected their staff groups to a Zero-Base Budgeting (ZBB) effort. This system of budgeting analyzes and evaluates existing operations and programs as if they were new activities. There is no reference to the current or prior years' budgets. In essence, the zero-base budget is based on "a fundamental analysis of the objectives, goals, and purposes of the organization and the resources required to achieve such goals."[1]

Here is how the two planners describe their experiences:

"The most structured staff planning we attempted was a 'zero-based' planning effort. It tried to define activities of staff units, resources required, alternate ways of providing the activity, and benefits from the activity. The system was a paper monster, and required a great deal of management time. With all the detail it was too easy to use up time reviewing individual 'trees' rather than the 'forest.' "

—*A glass products manufacturer*

* * *

"An effort was made five years ago to institute zero-base budgeting for staff groups. The groups that did the exercise seriously benefited greatly from the enhanced knowledge of their contributions and costs. However, budget approvals were made largely independently of the plans as presented (in the framework 'I don't care what they say, they will only get $X'). The result was the general disillusionment of those doing good plans. The system was not tried twice."

—*A building products service company*

[1] From William G. Droms, *Finance and Accounting for Nonfinancial Managers*. Reading Mass.: Addison-Wesley Publishing Co., 1979, p. 134.

---

those functions prepare a written functional support plan."

When Plans Are Not Required

Those companies in the survey that do not require their staff units to prepare plans generally attach little importance to this kind of planning in the larger framework of business unit or corporate plans. Indeed, several say their companies have never done it, and apparently have not considered doing it.

Staff units state objectives in writing at the beginning of each fiscal year in an industrial products company, but, its planner states: "The basic goal of the strategic plan is to seek competitive advantage in the markets in which we compete. This certainly is an impossibility for the corporate staff department."

There are also companies represented in the survey that have had staff unit planning in the past but that have abandoned this requirement for one reason or another. Some believe that the benefits received are not worth the effort expended, citing a number of problems involved in the process.

A pharmaceutical company that claims to have had a fruitful and productive experience with its corporate staff unit planning has discontinued this practice for other reasons. Two years ago, the planning executive says: "We determined that no strategic issues for the staff existed, and thereby eliminated the task." He adds: "Once the major strategic issues are resolved (in our case, moving toward a much smaller corporate staff in a decentralized context), I believe that staff unit strategic plans are of lesser value."

Chapter 2
The Staff Unit Planning Process

It is difficult to generalize about the staff unit plans and planning practices of the companies participating in this survey, not only because of the differences in terminologies employed by different companies, but because each company may have its own variety of organizational requirements. For example, a company may require strategic plans from corporate-level staff units, but operational plans only, or no plans, from the division staffs; or it may ask only selected staff units to provide plans.

And although many firms integrate the plans into the overall corporate plan, in other companies there is only an informal check for consistency. Further, some organizations do not require staff units to prepare plans every year, but only on occasion.

Types of Plans Required

Most of the companies where corporate staff units prepare plans say that these are basically operational plans. Twenty-three of the fifty-seven companies that distinguished between the types of plans also ask for strategic plans from some of the units. Just four companies say they require only strategic plans at the corporate level.

But the phrase "operational plans" covers a variety of practices. In some companies, a one-year budget is sufficient, or a budget and a head count. In others, the goals of the unit are asked for, and a program of the action steps to achieve them is included. One respondent says his company's plans are basically operational, "but they are a great deal more substantive and subjective than simply budgets."

In addition, there are times when companies may ask staff units that prepare only operational plans to respond to certain strategic issues facing the corporation, thereby considerably altering the usual nature of the plans. In one manufacturing company, for instance, the plans prepared annually are primarily tactical, according to its planning executive. "However, in those areas where a change of scope is desired, or where the environment is changing substantially, a strategic planning document is prepared which outlines the longer term strategy and operational philosophy of the staff unit."

Both strategic and operational plans are prepared by corporate staffs in a chemicals company. "The strategic plans are functional (corporatewide), and the operational plans are for the corporate staff department itself." The planning director continues: "These plans are called Staff Function Direction Papers. After the initial issue, they need only be prepared when staff department management wants to nominate a change in the strategy for the function—and achieve corporate consensus on the new strategy."

Most operational plans have a one-year time horizon, but some extend to three years; strategic plans usually cover five years, according to most of the planners surveyed. In longer term operational plans, the distinction between operational and strategic may blur. The planner for a large diversified manufacturer explains:

"Operational plan has many meanings, depending on the group for which it is written. One significant factor is the time span of the plan. All units must do a one-year plan, which is primarily a budget but also includes the planning of actions to be taken in one year. A long-range operational plan is done more on an as-needed basis, depending on the nature of the unit and whether it is meaningful. Frequently a long-range operational plan will be required to support a specific business strategy."

Several planners say that the staff groups' involvement in planning is, or should be, limited to the assistance they give to operating units in the development of their plans. This may call for the submission of annual goals or objectives for the staff units, sometimes under a management by objectives (MBO) program. An insurance company asks for monthly written MBO statements from its staff groups, for example, and strategic issues that arise are discussed as appropriate or needed. Issue papers, but not written plans, are prepared as part of that process.

Scheduling and Integrating Staff Plans

The problem of preparing staff unit plans vis-à-vis divisional or corporate plans gives rise to the traditional chicken-egg syndrome, several planners assert.

"It's hard to develop a plan without knowing what the need is going to be," observes a manufacturing company's vice president of planning, "and hard to define the need until all of the demands for resources are added up and balanced." And the planning director of a publishing company comments: "Service departments cannot plan fully without having input from operating departments."

Three-quarters of the survey participants whose staff units write plans schedule simultaneous preparation in the planning cycle with the line units. This compromise solution is defended by two planners, whose support group plans are prepared in tandem with operating groups:

"The rationale for the concurrent schedule lies in the belief that a strategic plan is incomplete without a feasible, agreed-to set of implementation plans. Further, the functional support plans and the strategic plans serve as a base for the annual budgeting process and, thus, should be completed prior to the start of the annual budgeting process."

—*An industrial products manufacturer*

* * *

"Proponents of 'parallel preparation' argue that (a) business unit strategies, once developed, change very little from year to year, and (b) staff departments are in close touch with business units anyway."

—*A department store chain*

The concurrent preparation of plans demands a high degree of communication and coordination between the staff units and the business units or corporate level. This is necessary to insure that staff services are adequate to support operating plans or strategic plans. A bank planner reports that a coordination process enables staff units to meet with their line counterparts prior to beginning the annual planning process "to exchange relevant information—and to insure compatibility of planned efforts between line and staff." He goes on: "In the final stage of the plan preparation, an 'interdependence chart' is prepared showing the anticipated interaction and support responsibilities, by department. The individual action plans also note this interaction and are checked for compatibility."

Most of the remaining quarter of the companies in the survey report that staff unit plans are prepared after the business unit or corporate plans. Even here, however, much coordination is needed in order that the plans be compatible.

At one bank, support department strategic plans are prepared after business unit plans but before the overall corporate plan. "It has been our practice to identify during the line business-unit planning process those plans that have a direct impact on a support department, and to pass this information along to the appropriate support area. Corporate Planning functions as a liaison in this process to ensure that the support departments are apprised of line department plans that have implications for their activities. We find such timing of support department planning to be preferable," the planning vice president says, "because it allows for the integration of line department needs early in the support department planning process."

Only two companies state that staff plans are prepared before the other unit plans. One of these, a bank that tried this for the first time, reports on its experience:

"Historically, staff unit plans have been prepared simultaneously with the profit center plans. This year, we experimented by preparing the cost center (staff unit) plans first. It was not entirely successful, because it was difficult to review staff budgets in the absence of any understanding of the levels of expected corporate profits."

The staff unit plans in most of the companies participating in this survey are integrated into the larger business unit plan or overall corporate plan. In order to be effectively integrated, however, staff plans have to provide information that is relevant to, and compatible with, the larger overall plans. A number of companies try to design the format of the plans to expedite integration. (See Chapter 3.) Frequently, the requirements for staff unit plans parallel those for operating unit plans; indeed, several companies use the same plan format for both operating and staff units, with slight revisions for the latter groups.

Most often, the planning department acts as integrator and coordinator. In fact, this is one of the major responsibilities of many corporate planning departments.[1]

A number of companies, however, say that they have no formal integrative process. In some cases, staff plans are integrated for budgetary purposes only, or are not integrated at all into any larger plan. A diversified products manufacturing company's planner comments:

"Staff unit plans are prepared simultaneously with the business unit plans. All are reviewed by the corporate management committee. While this is a formal review, the integration is more informal than formal. The major staff services are tailored to and utilized by the operating divisions. So integration takes place more on an operational face-to-face basis than through some formal pro-

---

[1] See Rochelle O'Connor, *The Corporate Planning Department: Responsibilities and Staffing,* The Conference Board, Report 806, 1981.

Exhibit 1: Planning Process Suggestions for Corporate Staff Departments—A Food Company

Below are suggestions for your use in developing your department's Three-Year Plan:

A. **Planning Steps**

   Your own personal experiences over the last four years have given you a firsthand knowledge of some of the steps successfully used in a good planning process—you should consider following similar steps in your department's three-year planning.

   1. *Participation:* Identify the managers and professionals in your department who can contribute, provide the atmosphere and mechanism to allow participation and contribution. Consider scheduling department three-year planning meetings. Encourage participation using those methods which are best suited for your department.

   2. *Preparation:* Use written assignments to provide a means for your associates to commit themselves to what is on their minds. For example:
   — One assignment might ask for an independent, written appraisal of department strengths and weaknesses.
   — Another might ask for the identification of current activities which have become obsolete. One sure way to increase the overall effectiveness of your department is stop doing those things that are not contributing to the accomplishment of the corporate strategic objectives and your supporting three-year objectives.

   3. *Qualitative Objectives:* The *driving force* of every plan must be the *qualitative objectives;* the *precise statements defining* the *results* which *you expect to achieve.* Each objective can then be supported by one or more action plans, which are designed to contribute to the accomplishment of the objective. Concentrate your and your associates' personal time, thought and effort toward the definition of these major qualitative objectives and the supporting action plans.

B. **Department Services—Support to Divisions**

   Every corporate department is providing critical services and support to the divisions. The quality of those services is an important measure of your department's performance.

   Your department's Three-Year Plan must consider both the current and future allocation of department resources in support of the operating divisions.

C. **Corporate Staff Departments—Interdependence**

   To insure unity of corporate direction and the addressing of the corporate key issues, each corporate staff department Three-Year Plan must be developed with full recognition of the interdependence among the corporate departments.

   This interdependence dictates that you continue to maintain open communication and coordination with the other corporate staff departments to insure that your three-year objectives and actions are fully supportive and compatible with the three-year objectives and actions being developed by the other departments.

   It will be *your responsibility* to set up the necessary schedule to sit with the other corporate staff department heads to insure the following:
   — Your plan addresses those *action plans* that are necessary to fully *support* each of the *other staff departments.*
   — You have identified the support *your department* will require from each of the *other staff departments.*

D. **Reference Points**

   1. *Corporate Strategic Plan:* The reevaluation of the corporate strategic plan will be completed in early April, 1981, and you will receive a copy of the revised plans on or before April 16. Your Three-Year Plan should identify the resources required for those action plans undertaken to support established and/or new strategies starting in 1982 and/or 1983, and revisions to action plans now under way in support of those strategies.

   2. *Your Current Three-Year Plan, 1981-1982-1983:* Study and evaluate the objectives and action plans in your current Three-Year Plan. Critically appraise those objectives and action plans relative to your performance toward accomplishment. Are you planning and doing the *right* things? Are you doing the *right* things *right*?

   3. *Your 1981 Annual Plan:* With 20 percent of 1981 behind you, it is an appropriate time to objectively/critically ask yourselves, "How are we performing against our 1981 objectives?" What changes must be introduced in the balance of 1981, 1982, and beyond, to insure the accomplishment of the programs in support of the strategic objectives and strategies?

   4. *Divisions' Strategic and Three-Year Plans:* To correctly define the future needs of each division for your department's support services will require a careful review of the divisions' reevaluated strategic plans (copies will be available on or before March 9, 1981), and the divisions' current Three-Year Plans.

cess linking the strategic staff plan and the business unit plan."

To facilitate integration and compatibility of plans, many companies attempt to stimulate strategic thinking and educate staff directors in the intricacies of corporate planning. Some planning directors make the most of the opportunity presented in the issuance of planning guidelines and instructions to orient staff managers to the company planning process and to the principles and jargon of planning. Exhibit 1, for example, shows how one company introduces the planning cycle to department managers and offers suggestions for developing the plans. It emphasizes the need for communication among staff departments and for addressing the needs of operating unit plans.

Other companies may offer guides and instructions that include glossaries or definitions of planning terms, examples of the kind of input requested, or easy-to-understand explanations for each of the items required in the plan.

The planning calendar, of course, is a mechanical device for easing the integration of staff and operating unit plans. By establishing a schedule of dates to assure the timely completion of tasks by the various units, the planning exercise is synchronized to facilitate its course. An example of such a calendar for the planning cycle is shown in Exhibit 2.

Measurement Criteria for Staff Unit Plans

When no quantitative objectives are provided in operating unit plans, most of the survey participants agree, it is difficult to establish measurement criteria for staff unit plans. Primarily, the goals that are developed by staff units for their specific activities vary widely in character and do not necessarily present any measurable aspects. In addition, these groups are subject to unforeseeable and uncontrollable demands of operating units, which may considerably alter the plans that were developed. Small wonder, then, that the representative of a health-care institution reports that the managers of staff units "maintain that their contributions to the corporation cannot be measured in the same way as line units, either because of the nature of their work or because they are 'response' units, serving a clientele and demand over which they have no control."

This is a frustrating situation for many planners, who recognize the problem but have difficulty resolving it. Some report that no measurable criteria are set in their organizations.

Exhibit 2: Schedule of Planning Cycle—A Hotel and Restaurant Chain

Feb. 9, 10, 11	Senior management kickoff meeting.
February 26	Five-Year Plan instructions and economic forecast issued to operating groups by Corporate Planning.
Week of April 6	Staff departments to review the operating groups' strategic objectives to be included in their five-year plans.
April 9	Staff five-year plan guidelines issued.
April 24	Staff departments to submit to senior management a statement of their "Fundamental Purposes" and a statement of the "Objectives" to be addressed in their five-year plan submission.
May 4	All planning units to review their preliminary financial projections with Corporate Planning.
May 8	Corporate Planning to review with senior management the consolidated preliminary financial projections and determine direction for revisions.
Week of May 11	Corporate Planning to review the types of necessary revisions to the preliminary financial projections with all planning units.
May 22	All planning units submit final plans to Corporate Planning.
June 4	Corporate Planning to review final consolidated financial projections with senior management.
June 11, 12	Five-year plan wrap-up meeting.

"By their very nature," claims a machinery manufacturing company's planner, "staff groups do not lend themselves to measurement to the same extent that operating units do. However, to maintain integrity in the planning and goal-setting process, some form of measurement is necessary."

Several planners admit that, despite their efforts to establish measurement criteria, evaluation can only be subjective for many staff plans. An oil company respondent says of his company: "Evaluation criteria are not normally preestablished in the planning stage, but are adapted to the results of the plans and to the circumstances surrounding their implementation." Another planner comments that corporate staff programs are more "subjective" and generally call for "the *study* of new markets or products, or the *development* of new products, technologies, services, and so on." These do not lend themselves easily to measurement.

Such considerations present some respondents with a quandary of variations in measurability among staff units. A forest products firm's planner observes that the activities of some units "are easily measurable, like completing engineering on a project, or recruiting a certain number of accountants, while others are more subjective, like avoiding adverse public relations or assisting the businesses in strategic planning."

Another manufacturer says: "Plans dealing with those staff functions that are either completely centralized (i.e., treasury, taxes, legal), or are government-mandated or directed (i.e., financial reporting), are frequently easier to evaluate than are those areas that are 'softer' and thus more difficult to measure (i.e., communications, governmental affairs, planning, and some areas of human resources)."

There are typically, however, quantifiable measures for some of the objectives developed in staff unit plans. A common measure is based on a unit's expenses and costs in relation to the budget approved for the unit. These are, of course, readily obtainable figures, and, in many cases, this is the only kind of measurement applied to staff plans. Another quantifiable objective is the workforce goal: Head counts are easily available.

Another common measure is time-based. Adherence to projected schedules and completion dates for programs can be determined in most cases. "Usually a number or a date is forced into each plan at any point where it is meaningful," in a diversified company that "always tries to provide measurement features that are as specific and quantified as possible in any plan."

Other measurable objectives mentioned by the responding planners are those that emphasize improvements in efficiency and productivity. Some of these may be numerical; others may be rated by the fact of their achievement, or nonachievement. (See box.)

Five survey participants report that their companies have management by objectives (MBO) programs in

---

Examples of Measurable Objectives for Staff Unit Plans

Human Resources

• Maintain corporatewide employee turnover below 25 percent between 1982 and 1984.
• Hire engineers at a rate of twenty per year for five years.
• Run three-week training course on new procedures in August, 1982.
• Reduce minority turnover by _____ percent from _____ percent to _____ percent.
• Increase number of women in management from _____ women to _____ women.

Data Processing

• Attain on-line computer uptime of 98 percent by 1983, up from 96.5 percent in 1981.
• Achieve a scheduled work load to capability ratio of _____.
• Limit the average data entry cost per 100 records to _____.

Public Relations

• Obtain a _____ percent improvement in customer perception of nuclear energy within the service area.
• Place the CEO on a key policymaking committee of an industry trade group.

Purchasing

• Finalize new volume-buy contract with ABC Company by December, 1982.
• Attain a 20 percent reduction in cost of material.

---

which staff managers are asked to identify goals to be achieved for the year. These goals are usually established at about the same time as annual plans are prepared, and offer an effective method for measurement, some say.

One planner describes his bank's experience with a less common method of evaluation by the support groups' users:

"Each staff planning unit is asked to list the services it provides to other units, that represent 80 percent of its budgeted expenses for the coming year. The services must be described and justified.

"Because cost center costs are allocated to users, the cost centers are told to identify the five users that absorb the most cost of that cost center's services. *Users* are then required to rank the services provided to them on three bases: (a) quality, (b) relative importance of service to users, and (c) user value received per dollar spent.

"Because followup is not done particularly aggressively, there is not much incentive to improve the measurement technique of staff units."

Chapter 3
Contents of Staff and Support Unit Plans

THE INSTRUCTIONS and plan formats submitted by contributors to this survey indicate that most staff unit plans have the elements commonly found in corporate or business unit plans, namely:

- Mission statements, fundamental purpose, strategic thrust
- Objectives, goals, results expected
- Strategies, action plans, programs, projects
- Resources required: financial, manpower, time, equipment or facilities.

Exhibits 3, 4 and 5 illustrate the contents of plans for three companies' staff units.

This commonality is not surprising. If for no other reason, it reflects an attempt to impose a degree of uniformity on the many written plans senior management will have to examine.

Yet the elements often have distinctive meanings for staff units as against operating units. For instance, a "strategy" for a cost center is far different from that for a profit center. Staff plans tend to focus on the actions to be taken by the unit to fulfill its performance objectives, rather than on the implementation of a grander scheme of gaining or holding a position in the market and competitive environment. Exhibit 6 shows how a chemicals manufacturer explains the relationship among objectives, goals and action plans to its staff managers for planning purposes.

In the end, the elements of a staff unit plan are supposed to answer the same basic questions that they do in an operating unit plan. For instance, objectives pertain to what are you going to do; strategies, to how are you going to do it.

Most Common Items in Plan Contents

Mission statement. In staff unit plans, such a statement, by whatever name—fundamental purpose, strategic thrust, function—typically defines the purpose served by the staff unit, the scope of the activities it engages in, its relationships to other units in the organization, and, sometimes, the unique characteristics of the staff group. It is, in other words, a definition of the activities or services to be provided by the unit, and to whom. A hospitality firm's instructions on this element of the plan are shown in Exhibit 7. Other examples may be found in Exhibits 3 and 5.

Objectives, Goals and Results Expected. The objective or goal to be attained by a staff unit illustrates one of the fundamental differences in planning by line and staff groups. Whereas *measurability* is one of the most prevalent characteristics of an operating unit's goals, it presents a difficult problem for many staff units, as noted in the previous chapter.[1] In the instructions issued to staff and support units on this part of the plan, a number of the participating companies direct these units to develop objectives that are achievable for the specific function of the staff department, and for which it can take appropriate actions. For example, one company advises corporate staff groups to state objectives that suggest the following actions:

- "Capitalizing on existing strengths and underutilized strengths;
- "Developing new applications for unutilized strengths;
- "Improving weak skills;
- "Transferring responsibility to other planning units (other corporate staff groups or operating groups);
- "Delegating responsibilities to lower, more practical levels."

Other directives may inquire about the results or benefits anticipated from the proposed objectives. These may address particular problems or opportunities, and

(text continued on page 18)

---

[1] For a full discussion of objectives and goals in corporate planning documents, see Rochelle O'Connor, *Corporate Guides to Long-Range Planning,* The Conference Board, Report 687, 1976, pp. 65-71.

Exhibit 3: Instructions for Completing Integrated Plan for Staff Groups—A Wood Products Manufacturer

I. GROUP OVERVIEW

  A. EXECUTIVE SUMMARY

  Summarize your plan. Emphasize the critical issues facing you over the planning period and share, from the group executive's perspective, which issues in this plan you are personally most concerned about.

  B. MISSION

  Define the mission of your staff group during the planning period as it relates to the company's strategic objectives. Briefly discuss such issues as:
  — Unique contribution the staff group makes to the company;
  — Purpose of function at the corporate level and throughout the company;
  — Interrelations with other staff functions and line operations.

  C. ENVIRONMENTAL ISSUES
  1. Of those components of the external and internal business environments that will have a *significant* impact on your group's activities, specifically delineate their expected effect. Such components might include:
      — Governmental laws and regulations;
      — Social attitudes;
      — Economic conditions;
      — Activities of competitors;
      — Changes in mix of businesses (i.e., acquisitions, new plant additions, divestitures, etc.).
  2. Review your current and future organizational alignment (within corporate headquarters as well as operating groups or divisions). Outline resource requirements and basic operating policies within your area of responsibility. Review strengths and weaknesses given the environmental issues in terms of:
      — Organization structure;
      — Management depth and flexibility;
      — Adaptability to changing conditions.
  3. Review human resource developments in areas such as those outlined in the Executive Review of Operations (ERO) instructions and comment on those issues that are viewed as *critical* to the accomplishment of your integrated plan.

  D. SUMMARY SCHEDULES

II. ORGANIZATIONAL AREA DETAIL

  A. DETAIL OF GOALS AND PLANS

  This section should include only those goals that are strategic, nonroutine and/or productivity related. Recurring, ongoing activities should be discussed in item B.

  Summarize your goals and plans in the following format:

  (1) *Specific goal:* State concisely and specifically what you want to accomplish.

(2) *Necessity*	*Who is Responsible*	*Timing and Expected Completion Date*
Define each goal in terms of: — Discretionary — Mandatory-government — Mandatory-contractual — Mandatory-executive decision — Formal approved strategy	Name those who will have primary responsibility for goal accomplishment.	Be specific by department.

  (3) *Brief discussion of how to obtain the goal.*
      (a) *Reason* for the goal, *benefit* to be derived, and a cost/benefit analysis on goals costing 10 percent or more of your total budget.

Exhibit 3: Instructions for Completing Integrated Plan for Staff Groups (Continued)

- (b) *How success of the goal is to be measured.*
- (c) *A general implementation schedule* which should include significant steps you will take toward attaining the goal.
- (d) *Alternatives.* Describe a *viable* alternative to accomplish the goal. *Specifically delineate the reasons why the alternative was not recommended.*
- (e) *Resource Requirements.* Identify additional resource requirements in terms of operating costs. Costs should include both incremental expense and allocated expense required to complete the goal. Incremental expense should include such items as salary, load, etc., for additional staff, computer support, outside costs directly related to the goal (legal or consulting), special travel reqirements, and so on. If the goal is not approved, this amount would become a net reduction in your budget. Allocated expense includes the quantified percentage of existing salaries and overhead that will be devoted to the accomplishment of the goal. If the goal is not approved, this amount would *not* necessarily become a net reduction in your budget. These resources should be specified as follows:

	1982	1983	1984	1985	1986
Incremental expense					
Allocated expense					
Total					

(4) Each staff group must have a productivity goal. Your goal summary should include the following:
- (a) A brief description of the measurement system and techniques being utilized.
- (b) A description of all productivity-improvement programs which have been in progress in 1981 and continuing in 1982-1986. Specifically include a discussion of progress, plans and programs related to the six basic processes to promote and improve employee involvement and participation in your group.
- (c) A statement of productivity-improvement goals for 1982-1986.

B. ONGOING FUNCTIONS

Summarize those functions that primarily involve ongoing activities and are not discussed in the goal section above. Please describe these activities in the following format:

(1) *Description of function:* Brief description of broadly stated function and related activities.

(2)   *Necessity*   *Time and Resources Involved*

Use definitions described in A-2 above.   Approximate percentage of total annual workweeks involved and resources used in performing the function. Resources should include the quantified percentage of salaries and overhead that will be devoted to the accomplishment of the function. Delineate the amounts by year as indicated above.

C. BUDGET SCHEDULES

III. ORGANIZATION OF INTEGRATED PLAN

A. Staff Groups Required to Submit an Integrated Plan:

— Corporate Secretary
— Finance Group
— General Counsel and Transportation
— Human Resources

Exhibit 3: Instructions for Completing Integrated Plan for Staff Groups (Continued)

B. Organizational Areas to be Included by the Staff Groups:

Human Resources
— Compensation and Benefits
— Corporate Medicine
— Employment and Administrative Services
— Labor Relations and Safety
— Organization, Personnel Development, and EEO

Finance Group
— Audit and Security
— Controller
— Corporate Planning and Development
— Risk Management and Retirement Funds
— Taxes
— Treasurer

Corporate Secretary
— Corporate Secretary
— Corporate Communications
— Corporate Contributions
— Investor Relations and Shareholder Services

General Counsel
— Legal (including Records Management, etc.)
— Governmental Affairs
— Transportation staff
— Transportation operations

Exhibit 4: Format for Developing Staff Department Plans — An Electric Utility

I. DEPARTMENT PURPOSE
   A summary of your department's role within the staff group with a listing of major responsibilities as you see them. Identify logical departmental subunits and attach organization chart (present and proposed, if applicable).

II. DEPARTMENT OBJECTIVES AND TARGET 1982 GOALS
   A set of objectives that your plan supports and at least one target 1982 goal for each objective.

III. ASSUMPTIONS
   A list of major assumptions that support your department plan; note any differences from current corporate assumptions.

IV. MAJOR PROGRAMS
   A listing of the major programs, present and proposed, and activities necessary to support your objectives.

V. RESOURCE REQUIREMENTS SUMMARY
   A summary of the resources expected to be required by the department in order to carry out its plan: give *summary* information for 1982 and 1983-1986 for (a) capital and expense requirements, (b) human resource requirements, and (c) facilities and equipment requirements.
   Identify external resource requirements, if applicable (e.g., consultants, other company departments).

Exhibit 4: Format for Developing Staff Department Plans (Continued)

VI. MAJOR PROGRAM OUTLINE

Include a completed analysis form (Attachment) for each major department program identified.

VII. HUMAN RESOURCE PLANNING

Include a listing of department's projected human resource requirements, by major category, for the 1981-1986 time period.

Final department goals will be established following board presentation of the 1982 plan and corporate budget in December, 1981.

**ATTACHMENT—
MAJOR PROGRAM ANALYSIS
1982 PROGRAM ACTIVITIES
STAFF**

Instructions for preparation of major program analysis are as follows:

1. Show department, cost-center number, and program number, if used.
2. Give descriptive program title.
3. List the persons responsible for the program. Designate high, medium or low priority.
4. Show program status.
5. State one or more basic objectives for the program through 1986 (e.g., what will be achieved).
6. a) State existing goals for 1981, if applicable.
   b) Propose target goals for 1982. Note: They will not be made final until December, 1981.
7. List the measures that will be utilized to track performance.
8. Give a brief description of how the program is or will be structured (e.g., how the objectives will be accomplished). Identify impact, if applicable, of program on other departments.
9. Show major milestone events, if applicable, and dates.
10. Give estimated program costs.
11. a) Give the justification for the program (why it is necessary).
    b) List the major assumptions on which the program is based.
12. List estimated manpower requirements (who will be involved). Divide into department, nondepartment (e.g., task force, MIS support, etc.) or outside (consultant and contracts) resource categories.
13. List facilities (building, floor space, etc.) requirements as appropriate.
14. List major office equipment or vehicle needs.
15. State any known constraints or problems that are (or may) prevent attainment of the objectives.
16. Evaluate the impact of feasible alternatives to the proposed program. Examples might be:
    1) Elimination of the program;
    2) Change in scope, schedule or priority of the program as proposed; or
    3) A completely different approach that would meet the same objectives.

Exhibit 5: Guidelines and Instructions for Corporate Staff Department Plan—An Industrial Products Manufacturer

SECTION I — MISSION AND SCOPE

Prepare a brief statement of the department's mission and scope of activities (approximately one or two paragraphs). The statement should indicate the extent of the responsibility as it relates to the operating groups and other staff departments.

SAMPLE

<u>Corporate Planning and Development</u>
<u>Mission and Scope</u>

To support and amplify the efforts of the chairman's office regarding improved strategic management throughout the corporation by managing and coordinating the corporate planning process; developing a corporate strategic plan emphasizing goals and selective commitment of corporate resources; assisting operating units in planning and business analysis; providing a corporate economic outlook and market analysis highlighting major trends that will have an impact on [our] businesses; and formulating a strategy for new business development, primarily by acquisition or merger, to achieve established corporate goals.

In fulfilling this mission it is important to maintain close coordination with operating group and sector management regarding the plan and the comptroller's office regarding coordination of the budget with the planning process. In addition, close coordination with corporate capital planning and research and development is critical to evaluate the commitment of corporate resources consistent with the strategic plan.

SECTION II — ORGANIZATION

Provide a current organization chart indicating direct reports to the department head and their major functional responsibilities. Also indicate the number of professional and clerical people assigned to each of the direct reports. Review any recent or anticipated changes in the organization.

SECTION III — GOALS

Short and longer range goals for the department should be established and priorities set with anticipated completion dates noted. Goals should be in response to recognized opportunities or needs for improved services and should demonstrate initiative for reducing unnecessary or marginal services and realizing cost savings to the corporation. Limit this presentation to a maximum of two pages.

SECTION IV — STRATEGIC PROGRAMS

Describe the purpose and explain the elements of any new programs being planned. Define the resources required for the programs in terms of personnel, outside purchased services, equipment rental, or other and the benefits anticipated from each program. Quantify the resources in dollar terms. Each program should be related to achievement of the stated goals in Section III. Limit this presentation to a maximum of three pages.

SECTION V — BUDGET ESTIMATE

Prepare an estimated budget for 1982 along with an updated estimate for 1981 expenses. Use the attached format, and explain any major changes being forecast. The resource requirements for new programs explained in Section IV should be identified in the 1982 budget estimate along with any cost reduction anticipated. If prior year's expenses are not comparable due to reorganizations, etc., please note.

Exhibit 5: Guidelines and Instructions for Corporate Staff Department Plan (Continued)

DEPARTMENT BUDGET
($000)

	1979 Actual	1980 Actual	1981 Budget	1981 Est.	Budget/Est. % Change	Forecast 1982	1981 Est./ 1982 Forecast % Change
Number of Employees							
Salary & Wages							
Employee Benefits							
Travel-Meeting Expense							
Occupancy Cost							
Communications							
Supplies & Services							
Equipment Rental							
Subscriptions							
Research Publications							
Consultants							
Seminar Expense							
Other							
TOTAL							

Exhibit 6: Definitions of Objectives, Goals and Action Plans for Staff Units—A Chemical Manufacturing Company

The terms *objectives*, *goals* and *action plans* relate to each other.

An *objective* is an aspiration to be worked toward in the future. It is unending, timeless and enduring, and stated in terms of some relevant environment that is external to the organization. It identifies *what* we want to do.

A *goal* is an achievement to be attained at some future date. It is a *specific* measurable milestone to be attained in pursuit of the organization's objectives.

- Objectives and goals should be consistent with the past directives of the management. The following considerations should be taken into account when defining objectives and goals:
    1. Higher service levels to internal "clients";
    2. Higher service levels to external "clients";
    3. Minimize operating expenses;
    4. Respond to [parent company] objectives or requests.

- *Action plans* should relate to at least one cost center's objective and goal. The cost center objective and goal to which the action plan is more directed should be indicated by putting the alphabetical letter designation of the cost center objective and goal in parentheses following the action plan.

Exhibit 7: Instructions for Developing Fundamental Purposes Statement of Staff Unit—A Hotel and Restaurant Chain

---

Fundamental purposes are reasons for the existence of a planning unit. These purposes should be defined in terms of services and beneficiaries and should be unique to avoid a redundancy of effort.

In identifying the fundamental purposes of a planning unit, it might be helpful to consider the following items.

Who are the primary beneficiaries of the department's efforts:

- Other corporate staff groups
- Operating group staff departments
- Operating group nonstaff departments
- Outsiders

The *unique* efforts of the department might be characterized by the following:

- Discrete needs or functions which relate to a publicly held corporation, and exist only at that organizational level.
- The corporate staff role of functional leadership, policymaking and innovation.
- The corporate staff role of audit or review.

Once the fundamental purposes have been identified, other nonunique functions could be identified as prudent because:

- Efficiency or quality improvement will result from centralizing a staff function.
- There is no overlap with operating group capabilities.
- There is no overlap with other corporate staff department capabilities.

It will be necessary for each planning unit to prepare a statement of its fundamental purposes.

(text continued from page 11)

may be expressed in either financial or nonfinancial terms. Some companies ask the unit to specify how its objectives affect other staff and line areas.

While many objectives and goals statements require time schedules, this is more often part of the strategy or action program portion of the plan, and depends on the individual company's plan design.

Strategies and Action Plans. The essential strategy-action details requested in most of the documents studied in this survey are a description of the action program proposed, responsibilities assigned for carrying it out, and the schedule for implementing it. The latter may consist only of dates for completion, but some companies require more specific breakdowns, such as milestone dates, program status (for carryover projects), and other measures for tracking the progress of the plan. (See the box on page 22 for an insurance company's quarterly review process.)

Other requirements, less frequently requested in this part of staff unit plans, are alternative strategies (and rationale for their rejection), priorities for the various actions proposed, and the kind of support required, both internally and from outside. The resources needed to execute the plans (discussed below), may be asked for at this point in the plan, or supplied later and separately.

Some typical examples of formats for this part of the plan are shown in Exhibits 8 and 9.

Resources Required. Almost all the documents submitted for this survey contain requirements outlining personnel, financial and time needs to implement the plans proposed. Annual budgets may also be asked for at this stage. In addition, some companies ask for facilities and equipment requirements, capital expenses where appropriate, or detailed costs for other items relevant to the company or business. The formats used by two companies are shown in Exhibits 5 and 10.

Less Prevalent Elements

Among the less commonly encountered contents of staff unit plans are two that are usually taken into account in developing strategies for corporate and operating units: (1) environmental analyses and assumptions that bear on the support unit's plans, and (2) internal assessment of the unit's strengths and weaknesses, opportunities and problems.

Environmental assumptions. Some corporate planning departments prepare and issue economic and environmental assumptions to all company units required to

Exhibit 8: Example of Format for Strategy Summary—A Bank's Data Processing Department

DEPARTMENT: Data Processing   GOAL NO. 3

RESPONSIBILITY: _____   DATE: _____

TITLE OF STRATEGY: Data Processing Education

PURPOSE OF STRATEGY:

Creation of a planned education approach to Data Processing

STRATEGY TYPE: _____ NEW   __X__ REVISION OF EXISTING STRATEGY

MARKETING THRUST:
- _____ Enter Into A New Profit Opportunity
- _____ Expand Present Market Position
- _____ Maintain or Defend Current Position
- _____ Withdraw From Business Segment
- __X__ Not Marketing Related

ACTION PLAN

Action No.	Actions to be Taken	Individual Responsible	Start Date	Completion Date	On Schedule Yes	On Schedule No
1	Develop education program specifically for entry-level trainees in systems.		10/80	6/81		
2	Prepare a new accurate job description for every position in DP.		3/81	8/81		
3	Provide education planning on an individual level for DP staff, including banking-oriented training.		6/81	12/81		
4	Develop training program for ongoing training of data processing personnel above the trainee level.		10/81	12/81		
5	Take skills inventory of all individuals in DP.		1/81	7/82		
6	Majority of recruiting for DP positions to come from training program.			6/83		

develop plans. In most cases, however, the unit is asked to prepare assumptions specific to itself that are of significance to its plans and that present potential opportunities or threats. (See Exhibit 3.) In a hospitality firm, for example, environmental issues are identified in the areas of operations, human resources, and consumer markets from which each staff unit is expected to determine the opportunities and threats applicable to it.

A chemical company's economic assumptions cover two periods: the next year, and the following three years. Its economic assumptions include prices of raw materials, energy availability, construction costs, interest rates, and so on. This firm also prepares "internal assumptions" for the same periods, which cover the organization of the company and salary increases. Another participating company also provides major internal assumptions for its staff units as a basis for their own unit plan assumptions; these include the corporate organization and diversifica-

Exhibit 9: Example of Plan Summary and Format for Monitoring—A Fuel Supplier's Public Affairs Unit

DECISION PACKAGE
EXCEPTION MONITORING SYSTEM

Activity: Public Affairs

Area: 213 — Corporate Communications

Status Indicator
O = On Target
D = $ Off Target
G = Goals Off Target

Decision Number	Decision Package Title	Decision Package Manhours	Decision Package Dollars	Major Outputs or Goals	Quarter, 1981 1st 2nd 3rd 4th
4150	MEDIA RELATIONS	2,895	$ 67,819	1. Conduct three electronic and print media tours annually. 2. Seek influential audiences for [company] executives to address and prepare appropriate speeches; supply number of responses and speeches made. 3. Disseminate news releases as topics occur. 4. Provide weekly executive news services.	
1158	FINANCIAL PUBLIC RELATIONS	1,568	34,390	1. Supervise production of 1980 annual reports and three quarterly reports. 2. Assist in security analyst seminar, produce analyst booklet. 3. Supervise preparation of financial and statistical update, stockholder information, and dividend reinvestment booklets.	
3150	INSTITUTIONAL ADVERTISING	200	3,670	1. Develop and conduct an effective institutional ad program.	
3155	ADMINISTRATION AND PLANNING	1,907	40,838	Goals not monitored in this report system.	
3159	SPECIAL ASSIGNMENTS	810	15,300	1. Prepare stories for [company] magazine; one story each edition.	
1900	AREA GENERAL	1,080	41,005	Area General decision package— no goals to be monitored.	
AREA TOTAL		8,460	$203,022		

tion program, financial factors, and personnel and staffing.

Factors that have a special significance in certain industries receive special attention. Thus, government regulatory and legislative assumptions—and the filing requirements they would entail—are prepared as "strategic critical uncertainties" for a resources company.

Here is how a chemical firm advises its staff units to prepare the "environment" portions of their plans:

"The *Trends* should indicate the past and future trends that will affect the cost center: including economic (e.g., transportation, communication, utility costs), governmental (political and regulatory actions), technological (e.g., computerization), and consumer (e.g., consolidation of divisional requirements) trends.

"The *Opportunities and Problems* should detail those trends or aspects of the environment which either present an opportunity (because of new cost center functions,

Exhibit 10: Manpower and Expense Forecast Form for Staff Units—An Industrial Engineering Firm

Staff Organization: _____ Section: _____

MANPOWER

NUMBER OF EMPLOYEES

	1977	1978	1979	1980	1981	1982	1983	1984	1985	1986
I. United States (total)										
A. Executives and Managers										
B. Professionals										
C. Technicians										
D. Clerical										
E. Hourly										
II. Non-United States (total)										
A. Executives and Managers										
B. Professionals										
C. Technicians										
D. Clerical										
E. Hourly										
TOTAL EMPLOYEES										

EXPENSE FORECAST ($000)

	HISTORY				EXP. FCST.	PLAN				
	1977	1978	1979	1980	1981	1982	1983	1984	1985	1986
a. Basic Activities Requirements										
b. Increments for New Activities										
First New Activity Expense:										
Second New Activity, Etc.:										
c. TOTAL										

areas of potential cost savings, improved service levels, etc.) or a problem (duplicated efforts, low service levels, etc.)."

Internal Assessment. In those companies that ask their staff units to assess their particular strengths and weaknesses, opportunities and problems, the emphasis is usually focused on the skills and expertise of the unit relative to what is required, or will be required, to meet the plan for the future. Proposed changes in the unit's key activities have to be considered here as well.

In some staff or support units, this type of assessment is critical. The data processing department, for example, must evaluate its capabilities, equipment and facilities for

An Insurance Company's Quarterly Review Process for Monitoring Staff Unit Plans

Originally developed to upgrade operational and strategic planning in the profit centers, the quarterly review process of an insurance company has been extended to staff units as well. The objectives of the review process, in which the corporate planning department plays a major role, are to:

"(a) Permit senior and top management a regular opportunity to review and assess the performance of departments against the goals and objectives established in their business plans;

"(b) Foster explicit consideration by senior management of the implications of performance results and possible departmental responses and actions;

"(c) Provide an ongoing mechanism for affirming or changing, as appropriate, departmental strategies, action plans, and strategy review studies in light of actual performance, changes in the business environment, and other internal or external developments; and

"(d) Enhance effective communication among members of senior management."

Briefly, the process consists of four steps:

(1) *Quarterly Report.* The participating staff unit prepares a summary report consisting of: (a) overall performance, including significant variances from plan; (b) business situation or environment changes since the plans were formulated; and (c) responses to significant variances from plan.

(2) *Joint Analysis of Quarterly Report by Corporate Planning Staff and Support Department.* This review identifies and analyzes those key business issues and decisions, together with other appropriate information, which may warrant top-management attention.

(3) *Issues for Quarterly Review.* Corporate Planning and the staff unit determine the issues to be presented for consideration, establish the agenda for the review meeting, and forward this, together with other appropriate background material, to top management.

(4) *Quarterly Review.* The quarterly reviews are primarily a means by which top management can affirm or alter the strategies and action plans of the departments in light of actual performance, changes in the business environment, and other developments. The meetings are action-oriented to leave participants with a sense that something has been decided and a clear understanding of what follow-up actions are necessary. The corporate planning unit works with the department to prepare summaries of the meeting, reflecting decisions made and agreements reached.

---

their ability to provide the services for which it is committed.

An insurance company's planning guidelines states:

"Identify and assign priorities to five to ten strengths and weaknesses of your support unit's ability to accomplish its mission (objectives and goals) relative to internal forces (other regional offices, resource allocation, etc.) and external forces (major competitors and/or the industry, etc.).

"Make sure your strengths and weaknesses are of significant importance. They need to be items that affect corporate goals such as profitability, competitiveness, growth, etc."

Chapter 4
Appraising Staff Unit Planning

REQUIRING STAFF or support units of the company to prepare annual written plans meets with mixed success, according to the 85 planning executives who responded to this survey. They are almost equally divided into pro and con camps in their evaluation of this practice.

Benefits Perceived

Basically, most of the planners who consider staff unit planning a valuable effort ascribe to it the advantages associated with the strategic planning process itself. Despite the vague objectives and lack of quantification sometimes found in staff unit plans, the planners cite a number of intangible, as well as tangible, benefits that make such planning worthwhile.

• *Increases management awareness of staff units.* The review of staff or support unit plans, respondents say, brings home to management the role, needs and contributions of these units, and this increased awareness often results in increased interest from management. Further, planning frequently forces an annual critical examination of the charter, mission and activities of staff groups, a review that might not regularly be accorded these functions. To this end, proponents of staff planning claim the plans show whether the projected levels of staff activities are appropriate to the specific operating unit and corporate strategies, and whether the individual units can support each other in the designated time frame. Several respondents also maintain that the development and review of these plans may provide an early alert to potential problems in the unit by exposing it to close scrutiny and thereby catalyzing corrective action.

• *Improves financial decisions by senior management.* The financial implications of support unit plans are more readily perceived, according to several of the responding panel members. It is important, many planners believe, for management to understand the consequences of approving staff units' goals and programs, to see where the staff organizations' dollars actually go. Projections of

---

Effective Staff Unit Planning in Two Companies

"Our experience with staff unit plans has been very satisfactory. Staff plans are equally as important as profit center plans. Our staff needs a clear statement of what is to be accomplished over the planning period and a formal commitment to complete the plan just as much as the profit centers. The staff plans make clear to the profit centers what can be expected in the way of support from the staff. Inclusion of the staff units in the formal planning process further promotes coordination and communication between staff and line units."
—*An insurance company*

* * *

"Staff unit plans have had value as a vehicle for communications among departments, particularly between the 'supported' and the 'supporter.' They have exposed to senior management the department head's vision of his role. They have focused attention on strategic issues, such as allocation of resources to systems and systems priorities in the company. They have highlighted the need for coordination. They may contain vital data for planning company performance and financing."
—*A retail chain*

---

operating expenses and human resource needs are almost always part of staff plans, and these frequently influence costs and profitability.

The planning directors of two companies explain how both the business unit and corporate staff affect the financial considerations in their strategies:

"The staff unit plans are important in our business unit planning efforts. The tactical plans for each business unit are entered into financial models to develop income statement and cash-flow information which is then consolidated for the corporation, leading to determination of corporate financing needs. Without information from staff units, dealing with manpower costs, equipment costs, operation and maintenance expense, and costs of administrative services, the business unit and consolidated plans would not forecast the company picture as closely."

—*A fuel supply company*

* * *

"At the business unit level, we feel that if meaningful strategy is to be made and implemented, the functional plans have to be tied in with it, and we look for these tie-ins in evaluating the strategies of our business units during the capital-allocation process. At the corporate level, such plans are helpful in deciding where to allocate our corporate staff budgets when we are in the usual situation of requests exceeding what we feel we can spend."

—*An industrial products manufacturer*

- *Promotes management development of staff heads.* Just as strategic planning is considered by many as a management-development tool—the journey rather than the destination being the aim—some survey participants believe that planning exercises in strategic thinking broaden the staff directors' horizons and improve the managerial competence of the heads of staff functions.

In this connection, some staff units are instructed to consider alternatives to their current direction and to ponder its longer range development. One large manufacturing company's planning executive, commenting on the improved quality of the functional support plans in his firm over time, notes their growing strategic focus:

"They are increasingly viewed as an integral part of the overall strategic planning process. We are encouraging each function to become more involved in the strategy development part of strategic planning. Traditionally, functional support plans have encouraged the functions to think that their role is primarily implementation."

- *Strengthens communications between units.* The planning process strengthens communications, not only between the staff unit and senior management, but also between line and staff, and between business unit and corporate levels, and among the various staff units themselves. Staff unit planning, many survey participants believe, also encourages all units in the organization to work in unison toward the achievement of corporate or business unit objectives.

Doubts and Drawbacks

For all the benefits of staff unit planning claimed by many survey respondents, there are as many drawbacks cited by those whose experiences have been disappointing.

- *Accorded minor role in planning process.* A number of participants feel that staff unit plans play only a minor role in corporate or divisional strategy. They describe

---

A Bank's Philosophy of Support Department Planning

"It has proven to be difficult to get support departments out of a posture in which they react to the needs of line business units (with the time lag and service gaps that inevitably are a function of such a posture).

"The principle that guides our support planning process is that, to the extent possible, support units should employ the same planning fundamentals as line business units do. Like line business units, support units serve an identifiable market offering a product or service that can be differentiated. Whereas line business unit planning addresses the issues of *how* to compete and *where* to compete, support unit plans address the analogous questions of *how* to serve the corporation and *where* to direct their resources. Through adherence to these principles and through better integration of line and support department plans, we believe that the quality of the support planning process will improve and that it can become a much more useful management tool."

---

them in various ways: "peripheral to overall corporate planning," "adjunct to mainstream planning," and so on.

A bank planning executive states: "The staff unit plans have been designed to support the business unit plans. One of the principal problems of developing staff plans stems from the perception by some managers that these plans *are* less important. The emphasis seems to be more on cost control and less on creativity."

"Staff unit plans will take a much longer time to be accepted in the corporation as compared with plans of the operational units," claims the planning vice president of an industrial products firm. "This is due in part to the fact that operational problems always receive a higher priority; and, in part, to the fact that the performance of functional units is not easily measurable and, therefore, the plans are more difficult to understand. However, we do find that progress is being made and that these plans are becoming more acceptable, even though only gradually."

- *Insufficient management commitment to staff plans.* There is a pervasive note of a lack of management commitment to staff planning—the sine qua non of any form of planning. Where management does not recognize the value of staff unit plans, they are usually doomed to neglect or abandonment. A grain company planning director reports that his company had introduced a planning system among the staff departments some years ago, which required the establishment of specific goals and objectives at the beginning of each fiscal year, followed by quarterly reports indicating progress to date. "But this system fell into disuse after a year or two," he says, "primarily because top management did not appear to use it as a management tool. In other words, nobody ever looked at the reports or took any action in regard to them."

• *Lack of planning expertise in support groups.* One of the strongest criticisms of staff unit planning voiced by a number of respondents to the survey is the lack of planning know-how in these units. This fault is exacerbated by the difficulties of developing appropriate guides and instructions for staff executives.

Among the problems are educating staff unit heads in planning procedures and introducing them to planning formats and reviews. This, of course, is a problem relevant to operating units as well, but for staff and support groups it often involves units with widely varying missions that have difficulty establishing common performance measures.

Moreover, staff units "require significantly more attention and handholding when it comes to developing plans than do operating units," according to one planning director. Another notes: "Many departments seek assistance of planning services to do their five years of numbers. They supply only very basic assumptions—changes in staff is about all they address."

Several planners also report the problems in forecasting the demand for the services these units provide. Changes that are not anticipated occur frequently, these panel members say.

The quality of plans submitted by support groups comes under considerable criticism by some executives. The "strategies" are "little more than platitudes," according to one, and they go into great detail on specific projects "with little perspective on the *need* for the projects or their priorities. Sometimes, there is no timetable, resource requirements, benefits, and so on."

An insurance company planner sums up the problems he has encountered with staff unit planning:

"1. Diversity of units leads to diversity of quality of planning and plan presentations.

"2. Technical and/or specialized background of some staff personnel inhibits communication necessary for good planning coordination.

"3. The more removed from current contact with the marketplace, the more likely the staff unit is to be less responsive to changes in strategies and programs requiring support.

"4. The failure in some cases to realize how the staff unit can support a particular strategy, or to be imaginative in developing support. We can determine if a project presented in plans is detrimental to strategies or is beyond current resources, for example, but cannot evaluate what is not there unless the absence is conspicuous."

• *Empire building in the staff units.* A common complaint concerning the plans of staff units is that they tend to seek expansion beyond what is considered desirable by management. A forest products company planner gives his experience:

"The biggest challenge is controlling the growth of staff units which are promoting their own existence. Charging back services helps, but sorting among priorities still requires involvement of high-level management. We are presently working department by department to analyze staff productivity and redesign the organization to fit the needs."